Leader That Makes Leaders

CONTENT

"If you can avoid ministry, avoid it as much as you can; if you succeed avoiding it, which means you are not called to it"

Bishop T.D Jakes.

"There comes a stage in ministry especially when one has remained faithful following God and heeding His instructions that every little effort seems to bring overwhelming result"

Dr Leo Ameh

CHAPTER ONE

INTRODUCTION

There are many errors that lead to confusion in life and ministry; among which are - doctrinal errors, moral questions, disloyalty to heavenly directions, wilful and blind pursuits of earthly things and family cases at the expense of spiritual pursuits.

The topic affects all true living ministers who aspire to be relevant in their divine assignment in these end times.

God wants us (young ministers) to escape the causes of disappearance of God's great men who have gone into spiritual oblivion while still alive. Those who have forsaken the pathway that brought them to the limelight, fame, glory and the pathway that made them great blessings to their generation. The pathway that made them God's chosen vessel, when they are called to the ministry. The pathway that made them a vessel unto honour. Those called in the past have lost touch with grace, power and realities of God's wonders, who are not relevant to God's plans, purposes, will and God's wonders, who are no more relevant to God's plans, purpose, will and God's glory. Those who have been discarded, abandoned and forsaken by divine mercy and are in confusion as to what happened to them (2 Peter 2:15-16). Having been persuaded by God for many years to no avail, like the prophets and children of Israel (Matthew 21:33-34, 22:37-39, 2Chronicles 15.2). Many cannot explain the genesis and cause of travails and down fall, many cannot explain why things are no more working for them, in their favour. They wonder what happened to them, why they see no more of their 'signs' (Psalms. 74:9-11) and fallen into spiritual and ministry dryness, instead of progressing they are experiencing retrogression, degeneration and indeed out of touch with contemporary moves of God, the grace to pray, wait upon and seek his face have vanished.

You try to console these ministers; they ask if God is still with them, why are all these things happening to them (Judges 6:13). They complain that God has forsaken them while they are the ones who have forsaken the pathway that brought them to greatness, they forsook their first love, loyalty, and integrity and all what God saw and put in them, they forsook God and His pathway (James 1:13-15, 2Chr. 15:2).

God showed me a revelation why he (God) always calls new people. In this revelation, God showed me how some of the people he called with joy and great promises with signs and wonders following their ministries normally abandoned him for their own selfish interests. Also in the revelation, most Pastors were seen playing games, politics and deviated to selling and buying; turning his purpose and divine plan and glory to shame through personal desires. While many of these preachers still preach, they have gone out of God's purposes and divine plan for their lives and calls. God has no option other than calling others to replace them, while they are there still preaching and glorying in the past.

King David Lamented and proclaimed "why are the mighty fallen and the weapons of war perished" (2 Samuel 1:1-27); prophetess Deborah answered that question when she said they choose new gods then, there was war in the gates (Judges 5:8, James 1:13-15). Jeremiah added his voice and said why should a man complain, a man for the punishment of his sins? (Lamentation 3:39 -47, Ps 78:56-54, 84:10-16).

There are many errors that lead to confusion in life and ministry; among which are - doctrinal errors, moral questions, disloyalty to heavenly directions, wilful and blind pursuits of earthly things and family cases at the expense of spiritual pursuits.

If we do not find spiritual and social solutions to these spiritual endemic and pandemic, we (younger ministers) shall be at the receiving ends. These senior backsliders seek to lead others astray after them. Like the old rejected prophet who led astray the younger prophet through false visions and deception (1Kings 13:11-32). There are many fallen heroes that want to disciple others after them, in spite of the fact that they are aware of their present situation with God.

It is not enough to be old in ministry but how relevant one is today is what matters. We must beware of the words of Christ that says "THE FIRST SHALL BE

THE LAST AND THE LAST SHALL BE FIRST" (Mtt 19:30, Mk 10:31) God's promise is that the righteous will still be fruitful in his old age. Billy Graham has been in ministry before I was born but he is still very, very relevant today, socially and spiritually having served for nearly 80 years in evangelism crusades. He is still being consulted, by the government of the day and the church leaders across the world. May we not be an abandoned project in God's hands and plans!

The aim of this book is to restore the withered hand, raise old bridges that have fallen, bring spiritual flesh and spirit upon dry bones and strengthen the younger generation to avoid pitfalls our fathers went through and to equip them for the great task ahead (Ps 78:1, 1Cor 10:11-14).

We know our God is a God of second chance, merciful and kind and ready to restore and reinstate and refurbish the prodigal leaders and sons who have gone astray through selfish, deception, satanic land mines that they have fallen into (Micah 7:18-20, Heb 3:17-18, Ps 90:1-17, Sam 3:37-40, Isa 55:6-7).

I remember God's mercy on an old Pastor that I preached in his church some years ago who had gone far away from his God and calling. He was confused and wondered where God was. He lost direction, he was in deep confusion as to what was happening in his life and ministry. But just one night of discussion brought revival and great restoration upon his life and ministry. To God be the glory, today he is doing fine.

God's mercy can still reach you no matter the depth of sin you have gone into, even if you stink in sins and disloyalty, God's mercy can cover your dirty past and bring new hope, new beginning, new focus and direction. It is not too late to come back. God's mercy is beckoning on you. During so many alter calls in the past some discovered they were in error, but they still came back to the Lord; it is not too late to come back.

There is hope for a tree if it be cut down by water; it shall blossom again (Job 14:7-9). The righteous fall seven times and seven times he comes back (Pro. 24:16-17, Ps 37:23-26). In this we hope our redeemer liveth (Job 19:25-27).

The biblical principles we shall share in this book will bring about self and spiritual recovery to all fallen heroes and heroine; and will strengthen, protect and fortify the young ministers to run and finish very strong (Gal 6:1, Gal 3:1-7). Also to warn the young ministers that the race has just begun, as to know that the purpose of this race is to finish well to win a crown, please the Master and never to be a victim of all the thorns on the way. **To heed Paul's warning to the Galatians that as we started well, we should end well (Gal 3:1-3).**

To start well does not mean one will end well. How we end is better than how we begin, though the foundation may be faulty but it has to be corrected because there is hope for a crucible foundation (Ps 11:3). The end of a thing is better than the beginning

(Ecl 7:8) Many that are first shall be last (Mat 19:30, Mk 10:31). Thanks be to God who has given us confidence, that he who hath begun good work in us will perform it until the day of Jesus Christ (Phil 1:6). Therefore he is also able to save them to the uttermost that come unto God by Him seeing, he ever liveth to make intercession for them (Heb 7:25).

CHAPTER TWO

PREFACE

RUNNING THE RACE WELL

"Not every service to the Lord is acceptable to God and Christ"

Christian Life and service is a race and like any other on earth, it has divine rules and principles guiding it. Hence it is impossible to run according to the rules and then be qualified or disqualified from the race (Heb 12:1-2, 1Cor 9:24-27, Gal 5:7). It is a race that has hindrances and obstacles (Gal 5:7, Heb 12) "you did run well or who did hindereth you from running well"Gal 5:7.

It could be run well or it could be run wrongly. Hence Apostle Paul determined to run well as to win the crown (1Cor 9: 24-27). There are carnal and spiritual hinderance that can prevent one from attaining the price (Heb 12). Apostle Paul decided to leave behind him some precious and valuable things so as to run well (Phil 3:7-10).

Even our services to the Lord cannot be done any how. It has wonderful rules and rewards of various degree, and qualities. Hence Christian services are divided into various degrees of qualities. Those qualified for different degrees of quality service and reward-able and inferior service due for disqualification and rejection on the last day of reward at the judgement seat of Christ (1Cor 3:9-15).

Not every service to the Lord is acceptable to God and Christ (Rom 12:1-2, 1Cor 3:9-15, Rev 3:14-18)

a. Gold

b. Silver

c. Precious Stone (1Cor 3:12b)

These are degrees and dimensions of qualitative services acceptable to the Lord. Below are the types of disservice unto the King of Glory and are due for rejection:

a. Wood

b. Hay

c. Stubbles (1Cor 3:12c)

Even our labour of love shall be tested and proved (1 Cor 3:12-13), we must prove our calling for acceptable, responsible and rewarding service that will win God's approval avoiding a degenerated labour due for rejection and disapproval (2Tim 2:20-21).

There were Pastors and Priests who lost out of these principles and were rejected (Zach 1:4-5, Jer 2:26, 23:11-43) both the ministers and their works were been rejected. The church of Laodiceans was threatened for quack service (Rev 3:14-16). Not every service rendered to the Lord, God accepts (Rom 12:1-2 Rev. 3:2, Jer 78:10).

"WHAT HINDERETH YOU"

Apostle Paul asked the Galatians Christians what hindered their running the race (Gal 5:7). The letters of Paul to Corinthians Christians explained what obstructed their journey. 1Corinthians chapter 10 explains how many of our predecessors lost out of the battle of life and service (1 Cor 10: 1-11). Verse 1-4, explained the benefits and privileges they had. In verse 5 he explained how and why God was not pleased with many of them.

Verse 6 and 11 expound on the fact that these actions are for our examples. Verse 7-11 worked on what disqualified them from reaching their goals. The Israelites in the wilderness are regarded as a church in the wilderness (Acts 7:38). Their Journey from Egypt to Palestine is regarded as a race and a type of Christian journey to heaven (1 Cor 10: 1-11) "PILGRIM PROGRESS". Many of them were lost on their way in the wilderness. **The purpose of this book is that we may be careful so that we may not end in the wilderness. We have our side of the bargain. Our responsibility so that we shall not fall from grace to disgrace** (Gal 5:1-4, 3:1-3).

In 1 Cor 9:24-27, Paul made known how he ran and the price he paid so as to run the race well. In Phil

3:7-16 he revealed the sacrifice he made. In Heb 12:1 he explained certain things or elements that we must keep aside, if we are to run this race well. It does not allow for overweight and excess luggage is not permitted, the road is still very narrow (Matt 7:13-14).

May we all run well successfully and not only in this world but to win the approval of our master for a job well done and never fall by the wayside (Matthew 24:50-51, 25:23, 2Tim 4:6-8, John 17:1-6). It is a known fact worldwide that many who started well majority of them ended up on the other side of the road. I once met a cobbler at an airport in Nigeria, who boasted how many countries of the world he went for the gospel but today has settled down or has accepted defeat. He could not explain why! 20 out of 30 fire brands of yesteryears are now in the cooler.

Let there be resurrection for the dry bones.

Amen and Amen!

CHAPTER THREE

"THE GLORY HAS DEPARTED"
<u>WHAT DOES IT MEAN TO BE RELEVANT?</u>

David served God and his generation till he died, (Act 13:36), even on his sick bed he was still being consulted.

It means to be of value to contemporary issues, to still be sought after, still effective, profitable, fruitful, dynamic and still being consulted for advice in contemporary spiritual, social and political issues.

To be a seasoned man of God, whose life and ministry's voice is still respected and still being sought for, to be in tune with happenings around, whose life style commands respect and fellowship.

Nothing is as painful as being alive and not relevant to contemporary issues, it is as good as being dead while living.

It is like a lion that has lost its strength and power Ecl 9:4. It no longer poses any threat to lesser animal who hitherto have feared it with trembling when it roars Ps 49:12-20, one's values has reduced and diminished, one could be described as a 'spent' 'force'.

A man who is relevant will be in tune with God and man, alive to the direction of the Holy Ghost, people will still seek for him/her for advice, will still be consulted, his opinions will still be respected and he will be still a fire brand.

He will command respect in the church, society and in his community. People will place a high level of values on his opinion, if this is not done, then the value to the church, it is saddening, this makes politician to fight back when they discovered that all patronage has gone, and they are no more relevant to political power. **David served God and his generation till he died (Act 13:36), even on his sick bed he was still being consulted.**

He determined and dominated his successor. Moses the servant of God served God until his last days on earth, nobody took over the leadership from him while he was alive.

He even took part in contributing to the making of his successor (Deuteronomy 34:1-12, his ministry lasted till last days on earth. Prophet Samuel lasted all his days and was relevant to the happening in Israel all his life.

1Samuel 7:15-17 though his children were rejected for being wayward yet he was still very much useful, respected and was highly held in honour and regard. God rejected King Saul while still on the throne; he was no more useful to God. God departed from him and it was proclaimed, **"Icabo** -the glory has departed," while alive 1Samuel 28:6. The ministry of prophet, dreams and urim's had departed.

His successor was anointed while he was still alive. 1Sam 16:1, show the beginning of Saul and the kind of favour he had upon his life and ministry. 1Sam, chapters 9, 10 and 11. You will see how he was rejected 2Sam 15:1-31. He lost his value as a King in chapter 17 of Samuel, the enemies began to oppress and suppress, and he became afraid because the glory had gone. He commenced a fierce battle against David. Read the last chapter of Saul on earth 1Sam 28:7. He sought for witches for help on the last day of his life and ministry,1Sam 28:1-18. **His ministry died before he died, Elisha's ministry survived him many years after he had gone.**

Samson was among the dead ministers while living, those ministers who lost their ministry while alive. Judges 17:20-21. He lost his anointing, his power and influence, he became an ordinary slave, the power had gone. Judges 17:20-21. God could not defend his glory upon his life (Isa 4:4-5). The defence of God's flood gate of the enemies (Isa 4:4-6). Normally God would defend his Glory upon His servants but in Samson's case, he could only be saved to die with the enemies.

There was another old prophet whose name was not mentioned though alive but his ministry had been replaced with that of a younger prophet. 1Sam 13:11. He was unknown in his community.

This is what we mean by dead minister, they are no more in demand, no more useful and profitable, they have gone out of the Lord; finished and have become a liability, burdensome for their families, church, and the body of Christ.   They are only left with 'yesteryears', exploits, no more genuine miracle, no more salvation experience in their preaching, no more joy of salvation.

Their preaching is more of storytelling that the acts of God. Lot was a typical example of this experience. He could not even save his wife and daughters in Sodom.

Judah Iscariot was in his category of people of God who lost their ministries while still kicking. Hear what was said about the foremost Apostle of Christ who saw, dined and witness Christ firsthand.

Act 1:16-22 "...*for he was* numbered with us and had obtained part of these ministry, now this man purchased of field with the reward of iniquity and falling headlong, he burst asunder in the midst and all his bowels gushed out".

Demas was in this category of servants of God who love this world (2Tim 4:10-11). Demas was no more profitable for the Lord towards the end of his life. When many men of God have been disrobed they run after titles to re-dignify themselves before people; like Adam covered his nakedness with leaves.

Elisha was such a great and mighty man of God whose power, influence and impact were intact even

to the grave. His ministry survived him for decades after his death. There are men according to the Bible whose work is still speaking many centuries after death (Heb 11:4). Paul an apostle was active, dynamic and resourceful till death. (Acts 28:22-31). The message of the Kingdom was very prominent and active in his last days of ministry. He was relevant until death, he finished strong and dynamic. Holy Ghost was still speaking to churches through his preaching and teaching (2Tim 4:6-8). He never watered down his messages because the world was resistant to his odd messages. He held on to the end. To some people, this trend is to fulfil the prophecy against the shepherd of Israel who God spoke against while alive - their prophetic ministry will be terminated and they will walk in blindness like ordinary people who never had an encounter with God (Ezek 44:1). It is called Ichabo- the glory has departed- the golden and glorious days of Israel has departed. GOD HAVE MERCY!

EVIDENCES OF REJECTION (Matt 7:16-20

There are evidences that God no longer walk with some ministers while still alive. That reminds me of a great man of God, twenty years before he died nobody heard of him anymore. He was on the sick bed in the hospital, nobody to pay his bills until he died. Nobody to bury him, they had to beg other pastors to donate money for his burial. Saul's body was left in the battle field for many days. Here are some of present day evidences of rejection. We must pray and walk in fear of God, so that we do not become a well without water; clouds that are carried with a tempest (2Pet 2:17).

1. Power for battle is gone (Judges 16:20-21, 1Sam 16). The fear of God disappears

2. The presence of evil spirit -(1Sam 16:14). Their spiritual gifts have been perverted.

3. The presence of God has departed (1Sam 16)

4. Anointing became history – once upon the time anointing – (Judges 16:18-21)

5. Defeat, defeat and defeat

6. Ichabo and disrobment (1Sam 28:25)

7. We see no more signs (Ps 90)

8. No more results (Ps 51)

9. No more answers to prayers (1Sam 28:5-6)

10. Boldness gone (1Sam 28:5)

11. Decrease and degeneration in grace. The love and affection of God's people disappear.

12. Broken fellowship with God (Ps 51)

13. No more signs and wonders (Ps 90)

14. No more fruitfulness and productivity (John 15:1-8, Isa. 5:1-7)

15. God no more defends his Glory (Isa. 4:4-6)

HOW TO HANDLE A REPROBRATE MINISTER:

We do not hate ministers in this category, we love and pray for them, however extra ordinary care must be taken. These nuggets must be followed:

1. Do not despise them - David never despised Saul

2. Pray for them - they need prayer for restoration (Gal 6:1)

3. Honour them, they were once God's vessels of honour

4. Do not argue with them it can cause resentment

5. Do not emulate them

6. Their counsel could be dangerous (e.g. the Old Prophet)

7. Learn from their failure (1Cor 10:11-12, Rom 15:4)

8. Avoid their laying of hands

9. Their mentoring could be dangerous (Matt 7)

10. Avoid their pit-falls

11. Meet their financial need and help them out of trouble (Heb 13:1ss)

Beware how the old prophet misled the young and vibrant, many ministers in this situation are Land-mine who set traps for young ministers through their counsels, mentoring and suggestions. One of the great men of God in America became a victim through the counsel a senior minister gave him to sleep with young women in his church. He advised, "Help them" it is part of it. Johnny, from then on he became sexually possessed and abused his members sexually.

CONCLUSION

To be relevant therefore; does not mean to be, necessarily in conformity with worldly standard, idea, or being on the fast lane; with church leaders who are crazy for titles; seeking attention or attracting attention to themselves and seeking worldly approval or men who boast of the glory in their 'yestyears'. Exploit, but have faded away today; but we mean to be a man/woman who is still very much up to date, useful, productive, profitable and a vessel of honour and still prepares for every good work and meet for the master's use in God's divine programmes. Still being a channel for the Holy Spirit and still bear's fruits in old age. Still having the Holy Spirit fire in his bones, who still has godly ideas that are valuable and useful to people in their lives. Men who still flow in grace and divine order. Who are still making acceptable impact to the Glory of God. Still loyal to God, His words, body of Christ, who still walk in obedience to God no matter the cost thereof. One evidence of relevance is found in Caleb's testimony forty years after he did a thing (what was the thing?), 40 years after he was still able to do the same. The fear of God is still intact upon his life. The moral testimony was still intact. His candle had not been put out and his oil had not run dry.

CHAPTER FOUR

WHY THE GAME IS UP

JUDGES 5:8, 1SAM 1:1-17

The question frequently asked is "why do ministers of God not last these days?" Some even died physically while some others died spiritually; while still alive but their ministry has gone dead. They are still alive and healthy, yet their ministry has become an obituary. We wonder why God the gracious and merciful God will abandon his anointed servants. How and why will he be provoked against his chosen people and abhor the people He redeemed and once 'cherished' (Ps 78:59). Why would God forsake the tabernacle of Shiloh his tent among his people (Ps 78:60) and delivered the strength of his people to captivity and his glory into the enemies' hand (Ps 78:61); 'handed over his people to the sword and rain ceased in their land' (Ps 78:62); He sent devourers to their land. He cut off their streams, the oasis run dry, and spring water blocked like the children of Israel whose fathers' journey to the promise land was cut short the wilderness (Ex 17:6, Num 14:11-34). They had lost their anointing and favour with God and men, fellowship with God they once cherished had become a burden. Their axe has lost its iron head (2King 6:5-6), their story became "once upon a time" (1Kings 13:11). They have a name that they live but they are dead (Rev 3:1).

King David was the first to ask this question, "Why, are the mighty fallen and the weapon of war are perish?" (2Sam 1:1-17). Prophetess Deborah answered that question when she said they chose new gods then there was war in the gates (Judges 5:8, James 1:13-15). Prophet Jerimiah added his prophetic voice 'why should a man complain for the punishment of his sins (Lam 3:39-47, Ps 78:56-64, 84:10-16). Under these heading we shall undertake a journey into why, and what make ministers to pack up their ministries while still alive. Here are some of the tragedies:

1. WILLFUL DISOBEDIENCE TO GOD'S INSTRUCTION (1SAM 15)

King Saul is a practical example of this fatal error in ministry, he respected and feared people more than God. When asked why he did what he did, his answer was too belittling of a man of his spiritual and political position; he was privileged to occupy, he feared the people, and obeyed the people and tried to bribe God with the fats of ram for sacrifice but God does not replace his instruction with sacrifice of any kind, "to obey is better than fats of rams and to hearken than sacrifice". Hath the Lord as great delight in burn offerings and sacrifices, as in obeying the voice of the Lord, behold, to obey is better than sacrifice, and to hearken than the fats rams" (1Sam 15:23-30), Prophet

Samuel replied, 1Sam 15:22-30. May we have and learn lessons from his errors (1Cor 10:6-12).

2. DOCTRINAL ERRORS

Both the past and contemporary church history is replete with sadness of how great men/ women were victims of doctrinal errors they contacted or originated themselves. Some of these great heroes lost their precious ministries to heresies.

As a young minister, I watched how many of these great men refused to accept correction for the errors they got involved in. Most of these early Pentecostal role models were once celebrated.

The bible being the book of prophecy, contains and predicted the information of yesterday, today and tomorrow; it predicts the events of today. False doctrines were some of the principal prophecies that will characterize this end-time ministries (Act 20:28-32).

Now the spirit speaketh expressly, that in the later times some shall depart from the faith, giving heed to seducing spirit and doctrines of the devil (1Tim 4:1, 2Thess 2:3). Note the following in this dreadful prophecy. Some shall depart from faith; they once preached sound doctrines of God but now have departed.

Giving heed to seducing spirit; paying attention; they once never have anything to do with seducing spirit but now are paying great attention to seducing spirit.

Many shall fall away from the faith, 2Thess2:3; they have been in the faith before. Some shall abandoned their first Love Rev 2:4, they have been in love before. False teachers with false teaching shall arise from among the church and shall lead many astray (Acts 20:28-32). I encountered a fruitful man of God in Lagos with false doctrines, he is no more heard of today. Though still alive he is no more reckoned with by men and God.

3. IMMORALITY

King David could still find favour to tell his story but Samson was not that favoured. He lost his anointing to a prostitute and died in process. Many God's generals lost their anointing to sexual immorality which today is extremely rampant among God's people. Judges 13-17 prostitute Delilah was Samson's undoing. One of the greatest sins in the church is immorality. Note:

i.   It is forbidden in the bible, Ex 20:14, Deut 5:18, Matt 19:18

ii.   Cultures of people do not permit it

iii. The society does not permit it

THE DANGER OF IMMORALITY:

1. It breaks marriage

2. It brings shame Prov 6:27

3. It destroys the future of children Isa. 57:3

4. It destroys love and trust

5. It causes un-forgiveness

6. It exposes the family to communicable diseases – HIV/AIDS.

7. IT BRINGS GOD ANGER:

   1. Lev 20:10 and Heb 13:14

   2. It prevents going to heaven 1Cor 6:9-11, Gal 5:19, Eph 5:3-5

   3. It defiles Matt 15

   4. It brings man to poverty Pro 6:24-26

   5. It brings loss of anointing 1Sam 14, 15, 16:30-31

4. <u>CURSES FROM BREAKAWAY SYNDROME</u>

Prophet Jeremiah was used by God to inform us that pastors can actually steal one another's sheep. "Behold, I am against the prophets said the Lord, that steal my words everyone from his neighbour" (Jer 23:30).

You Pastor a church, you are paid, housed while pastoring, only for you to be unfaithful and have ungodly desire to make away with the people. It is ungodly, and it brings curses, all breakaway churches have limitation upon their lives and ministry, history proves that church breakers have not fared well enough in ministry. Kenneth Haggin said, "The sheep you stole from another pastor does not belong to you and they will bring untold hardship to your ministry"; almost all who broke away have faced great consequences of their actions. They faced exactly what they did to their leaders – whatever a man sows that shall he reap Gal 6:7-8.

THE DANGERS OF BREAKING AWAY

1. It brings limitation upon your life and ministry

2. You will face the law of karma

3. You lose a great testimony

4. You will not trust your followers

5. You bring a curse of any kind upon your life and ministry (Pro 3:33 Mal 2:2)

6. It leads to dryness of anointing, favour and grace (Ps 45)

7. It raises opposition against you and your ministry in the future

8. It causes division in the body of Christ, which God hates (Pro 6:19)

5. INVOLVEMENT IN OCCULT PRACTICE

Many Pastors are said to be involved in this. It is a great sin in the bible both in the Old and New Testament. It has been found to be one of the causes of disaster in life and ministry. It is an abomination to seek for help from them, talk less of how much consulting them (Isa. 30:31).

6. <u>PRIDE OF LIFE</u>

Isaiah chapter 14, describe the danger and consequences of pride. Lucifer, Herod, and Nebuchadnezzar should be a practical lesson for all of us in ministry. Unfortunately today, many young ministers are growing without humility, which is the bedrock of Christian life and service. Pride is already judged, its destination is already determined. Lk 14:11, James 4:6, 1Peter 5:5 Pride goes before a fall, Daniel 4:37, Pro 8:13. Pride is the reason many people's anointing disappeared. To say the danger of pride is to be emphasizing the fact known to everyone. Lucifer was asked how art thou fallen, oh thou Lucifer? (Isa 14:12-15). King Nebuchadnezzar and Betsesa will be good classroom professors of humility, having had an awful experience of it.

7. LOVE OF MONEY

We do not need a prophet to tell us, the harm the love of money has caused in people's lives and ministry over the years, it is a plague to avoid with utmost carefulness (1Tim 6:10-11, Ex 23:8). Money was no evil itself but the love of money. Many ministries have lost their ministries when their attention were shifted to money for personal desire, this is what the man of God should follow: *1Tim 6 "but thou, O man of God flee these things and follow after righteousness, godliness, faith, love, patience, meekness"*. See the evils, the love of money has brought upon ministers who loved money? *1Tim 6:10, for the love of money is the root of all evil; which while some coveted after, they have erred from the faith, and pierced themselves through with many sorrows.*

8. <u>DEVIATION FROM DIVINE DIRECTION</u>

Apostle Paul called it disobedience to heavenly vision for many heavens have closed against them for the same reason.

9. <u>UNFORGIVENESS</u>

In practical term, un-forgiveness has its unforetold harm to one's life and ministry.

10. <u>DEVIATION FROM THE WILL OF GOD</u>

God has a divine blue print for each one of his people exactly suited to every one's peculiar need, enabling each one to make the most of his abilities. To deviate from this all important aspect of one's life is to spell doom. Jer 29:11, Jer 1:5.

11. DISCOURAGEMENT AND FEAR

When discouragement and fear come, faith disappears. God warned Joshua to beware of discouragement. Josh 1:7-9.

12.UNFAITHFULNESS

Gehazi lost his life and ministry to unfaithfulness; he was positioned for greatness in life and ministry but he lost all to unfaithfulness LK 16:10-13.

13.LACK OF WISDOM IN HANDLING SUCCESS

Success is good and it is God's will for our life but lack of ability to manage it brings danger and disaster.

14.WORLDLINESS

It is not only dangerous but a mark of apostasy. (1John 2:15-17, Romans 12:1-2, 2Cor 6:14-17, 2Cor 7:1). Because of worldliness, a lot of God's men have lost the power to pray and seek God.

15.LACK OF PRAYERS AND CONSTANT FELLOWSHIP WITH GOD

It leads to spiritual dryness (Isa. 40:28-30)

16.BUILDING THE MINISTRY ON SELF AND FAMILY

This principle provokes God to anger because that is not God's divine plan. Succession should not be a problem. Ministry is not a personal property. IT IS TRUST (Lk 19:13)

17.LACK OF EFFECTIVE ADMINISTRATION

Administration is a general problem in the ministry because many pastors do not care about the importance of it 1Cor 14:40. Many ministries collapse before their time because the total load of the ministry is on their head, there is no future for this kind of ministry should anything happen to them. The end has come.

18.LACK OF FINANCIAL MANAGEMENT

How money should be managed is not too detailed in the scriptures, however the bible supports wise spending and careful handling of it. There should be records of going and coming finance and how they are spent. Many ministries have collapsed because there is no diligent handling of money and careful record keeping; accusation comes in and there is no one to defend it.

19.LACK OF PROPER REST

Misuse of the body has a great implication for the users. Jesus told the disciples to have rest (Lk 10). Correct diets for young and old age is very important.

20.FAMILY PROBLEMS

Eli lost the priesthood due to his children. Samuel lost the priesthood due to his children. Divorce has destroyed many ministries today. Fight for the family was the advice of Nehemiah to his followers. Carry along your family was the advice of Joshua to Israel.

21.DELIVERANCE MINISTRY WITHOUT WISDOM

Using deliverance gift without wisdom is killing

22.FAILURE IN THE FAMILY

So many ministries are out of the ministry today due to family problem. These are the reasons why the games are up for God's general.

23.LACK OF GROWTH

Growth is a necessity; for one not to be outdated, he must grow spiritually, in knowledge, in grace, in character and in relationship with God and man. Lack of growth in these areas of life and ministry hinder progress in whatsoever one does.

CHAPTER FIVE

<u>KILLING THE KILLERS</u>

"For us to properly deal with these manipulations of Satan, we must be prepared for battle. It is a battle of strength, determination and total dependence on the power of God"

Apostle Paul mentioned that there were enemies in his days 1Corinthians 16:9. We cannot dwell too much on that today as there are more revelations on that now than in the days of Apostle Paul. We can only pray now that God will help us to properly locate those things that constitute downfall to ministers of God before us.

In warfare the first principle you will be taught, is never under estimate or under-rate your enemy no matter your strength or no matter how small the enemy is.

Secondly, proper strength, strategy, and types of ammunition of the enemies must be understood.

Thirdly, the principles of the warfare must be known, these things prepare your mind for the battle. Apostle Paul said, *"Less Satan should get an advantage of us; For we are not ignorant of his devices' (2Cor 2:11).*

He even told us who fights us, who the enemies are Ephesians 6:10-18. Apostle Peter told us how the enemies operated in his days 1Peter 5:8. Apostle Paul talks about the strength of our armoury 2Cor 10:3-6. That Satan manipulates men of God is an understatement, it is a general fact we are all aware of.

For us to properly deal with these manipulations of Satan, we must be prepared for battle. It is a battle of strength, determination and total dependence on the power of God to put Satan where he belongs before he gets us kneeling before him. Here are some of the ways Satan manipulated old ministers.

1. Pride

Success is sweet and has been vigorously pursuit by ministers in all ages. The fulfilment of this desire has also brought great danger to the ministers who eventually attained it. The success of David to want to know how many people he ruled. The success of Solomon grew pride in his heart. King Nebuchadnezzar was also destroyed for the pride of being the head of the worldwide empire. Lucifer was a typical example of people who cannot control achievement and success. Many successful ministers are victims of this "one thing" and have been swept off the way of God.

2. Immorality

The way that Satan manipulates the mind of many ministries both young and old is unprecedented in church history. It first began in the church in the wilderness where thousands of God's people died for immorality, 1Corinthians 10:1-13. **I do not want the judgement of God upon David for immorality. I do not want to end up the same way Samson ended. I do not want my heart to depart from the Lord like that of King Solomon. I do not want my ministry, and my family to scatter as we see it happen today among ministers.** I learn from the past 1Cor 10:4-11. Proverbs Chapter 4, 5, 6 and 7 warns us seriously about immorality. **It is said if 100 pastors gather, only about thirty of them may be freed from this sin. A lot of men of God may need to go for sexual deliverance.**

3. Love of Money

Money is a necessity of life, it is not a luxury. The place of money in life ad ministry cannot be over emphasised. It determines how much of an impact we can make; however, the care of it is the problem. **When programmes are held for how much it will bring in, then the love of money rather than the love of God and souls have taken charge. Men of God are seriously warned about the danger of the love of money, not money but the love of it** (1Tim 6:6-12)

4. Wilful Disobedience to God

Satan used people to manipulate King Saul to obey the voice of people than of God. Here lies the reason why many men of God are lamenting today...disobedience. **Disobedience has turned many generals in God's army to recruits,** it is our greatest undoing. How can a pastor or minister desire to do his own thing when Jesus Christ has no claim to his will but the will of God. Any minister outside the will of God, will have himself to blame for failure. **Every minister must yield his will to God's will, if he enjoy God's blessings upon his life and ministry** (Matt 6:9-10, Eph 5:17, Gal 6:6, Ps 40:6-8, Heb 10:5-9, John 4:34, 5:30, 6:38, 9:4 Matt 26:37 and 43, Lk 11:2, 22:42, Matt 7:21, 12:50, Mk 5:35).

The prophet used the children of Racabites for an example of obedient to Israel Jeremiah 35:1-11.

5. Worldliness

This word does not mean not having sufficiency or not being comfortable but simply means one living his entire life for what he can get for himself. **A little animal called a fox was used as an example - this little animal digs a hole on the ground where he lives - he fills this hole with all good things he needs and then closes up the hole. It will not be seen again until it finishes it stores** then it comes out again to refill its store =living for one's comfort - is worldliness - that is the idea of life of an unbeliever. Matt 6:25-36, 2John 2:15-17. When a preacher preaches for what he can get, that is worldliness; one of the dreadful tactics of the devil is worldliness (Matt 4:1-11).

6. Deviation From Ones Ministry

Saul was a powerful warrior until he sinned. He handed over his amoury to David, the armoury was too heavy for David. David decided to attack Goliath with what he had, he defeated Goaliath with his own armoury. A lot of ministers today ignore their ministry for a better one, hence the confusion today. We can adjust our manner of presentation for proper understanding and reception but we cannot let go of our ministry. The bible says everyone should abide by his calling.

Ephesians 4:1-3 2Corinthians 12:13 not everyone who preaches prosperity prospers and not every prosperous man of God preaches prosperity. Every vision has provision.

Every ministry has its own audience. If you lose your audience, the one you want may not accept you. Keep to your ministry. One of the attributes we should learn from Apostle Paul was his ability to abide by his call 2Corinthians 10:9-18). He was very proud and contented with his ministry.

7. Prayer-less Life

Prayer is the only way we talk to God and the secret of power of all men of God. Through it we contact power, anointing, direction and blessings. If we stop praying we lose power and all the benefits we desire through prayer. **It is a fact that no man of God falls until he stops praying. One of the things that kills the spirit of praying is "I have arrived mentality". I do not need to pray any longer. I have all I need so what is the need for prayers.** Prayers is like a throttle in a vehicle, when you throttle, a heavy vehicle will respond to the dimension of the acceleration. **Every ministry responds to the level or heat of prayer. Prayerlessness is one of the three ways the devil attacks the church.**

8. Doctrinal Manipulation

Apostle Paul caught this vividly when he instructed Timothy on the issues of the last days (1 Tim 4:1-4, Acts 10:17-31). The devil has three attack plans on the church and ministers, but the most grievous of all is doctrinal attacks. Church history shows that most serious issues the early church had, is doctrinal. It divided Christendom for more than (600 years) six centuries until Islam invaded the church and exterminated her in the whole of North Africa leaving a little fraction behind to struggle for survival. A lot of ministers of God like we know are today no more in the ministry due to doctrinal controversies that trailed their ministries until they are no more. Apostle Paul warned Timothy and elders of the church to beware of errors of doctrines that may grow among us.

Temptation for Fame and Power

Many ministers have died because they do not resist the temptation for power and fame, the same temptation came the way of Christ (Matt 4:1-11, Lk 4:1-11)

Broken Home and Family Life

I know a family highly anointed both husband and wife, very powerful for the ministry but their family life is nothing to write home about, they ended up in divorce, the husband now a driver and the wife remarried; the children are all wayward.

Bad Association

The infection of bad association cannot be over emphasized; 1Cor 5:6-9, 1Cor 15:3-34, bad association has killed many young ministers (Prov 13:13). God cares who your friends are.

Lack of Discipline and Integrity

Lack of integrity and discipline in life and ministry in these areas have destroyed many ministries 1Cor 9:24-27 and Phil 3:13 discipline and integrity.

   a. In life and ministry

   b. Financial matters

   c. Family matters

   d. Sexual matters

   e. Social matters

   f. Interpersonal relationships

Lack of Ministerial Ethics

Every profession gas its ethics. Pastoral ethics cannot be over emphasised. Omission of this has resulted in crisis. Interpersonal relationships among members of the body of Christ. Eph 4:1-3 most of what we ignore in ministry and life has resulted in little foxes that destroy the vine. The song of Solomon 2:15 'take the foxes, the little foxes that spoils the vines'.

Unfaithfulness, Rebellion and Betrayal of Leaders, Brings an End to Ministry

The successor of Elisha lost his future ministry to disobedience to leaders. The cost of rebellion is too painful to count. The causalities are too numerous to mention.

Overseas Ministry

Many young ministers abandoned in their countries of location for overseas, majority of these have turned to a paid job to survive, while their ministry is forever in the cooler. Many of these finally return only to discover their colleagues have become a household name in the gospel, but they can no more start afresh. Time was not more in their favour, just like Joshua could not accomplish his call because time was no more in his support Josh 13:1-7.

<u>The Deception of Sin</u>

Apostle James, the brother of our Lord Jesus Christ, revealed how Satan used sin to manipulate the downfall of many ministers (James 1:13-15).

1. The sin of divorce

2. The love of money

3. Pride of life

4. Lust of flesh

Sin has brought great reproach to many ministries. Paul advised the Hebrew Christians to avoid besetting in running their race (Hebrew 12:1). They are little foxes that destroy the vines (Songs 2:15).

<u>Unforgiveness</u>

Saul could not forgive David ever since he saw the hand of God upon him and an evil spirit possessed him.

CHAPTER SIX

<u>THE IMPORTANCE OF BEING RELEVANT IN LIFE AND MINISTRY</u>

How many politicians disappear after their office tenure and lose their relevance. Human nature seeks for attention and when God blesses a man, he gets a lot of attention from people. That is one proof that God called his servant. When Moses was called the people's attention was drawn to him. People gathered around Saul 1Sam 10:23-26. When Samuel was chosen by God people came from every part of Israel to seek for his counsel 1Sam 3:19-21. A group of poor people first gathered around David and then the whole tribe of Israel later came together to David. The crowd Jesus Christ pulled was one reason he was persecuted so much by the Sadducees and Pharisees John 6:1-2, Matt 4:23-24, Matt 9:35-36. People gathered around the judges, that they were so sure God called them. When a man is relevant he becomes the centre of attention for God's purposes, relevant to the destiny of God's people, the anointing is strong, functional and fresh, and he hears from God and fears God.

How to be Relevant

a. <u>Service; Acts 13:36.</u>

David was relevant till death, he served God till his last days. He served God and his people selflessly. The motive for the ministry matters, pure motive for service will help you to survive in ministry for long. **Service is the principal key to greatness** Mark 10:35-45.

b. <u>Keep to Your Ministry 2Corinthians 10.</u>

It is good to learn from others but to deviate from your call can get you out of ministry very early in life and get people's attention off you.

c. <u>Keep Pace with the Moves of the Holy Spirit</u>

The Holy Spirit is the administrator of God's purpose on earth and in the church you must keep obeying and following his instruction. 1Samuel 16, if you disobey the leadership of the Holy Spirit you are on your own. Moses and the people never missed the moves of the pillar of fire and cloud.

d. <u>Exercising Patience in Life Ministry</u>

The bible talks of patience in life and ministry, the bible talks of suffering and long suffering in life and ministry. God makes all things beautiful in his time, 1Peter 5:10, Hebrews 6:10, Hebrews 10:37-38

e. <u>Keep Professional Ethics</u>

Every professional has ethics that govern the dos and don'ts, so do the Christian life and ministries.

1. We must observed the moral codes,

2. We must observe the financial codes,

3. We must observe moral integrity,

4. We must observe General ministerial ethics,

5. We must observe interpersonal relationship codes.

f. <u>Godly Mentor</u>

The race cannot be run alone. You need support from men who have been there before you to guide you Luke 22:32, Lk6:40.

g. <u>Walk in Obedience</u>

Saul is a practical example for all of us to learn to obey God without problem. We should obey God's instruction without headache, if we should remain relevant in God's plans and purposes in this generation, Ps 81, Isa 41. David must teach us the importance of obedience Acts 13:22.

h. <u>Walk in Love</u>

John 13:30-35, those who walk in love remain the beacon of hope and aid to others.

<u>Abide in the Scripture</u>

Moses told Joshua to keep God's word and never deviate from it, for then shall he have a good success. Joshua 1:8-9. Studies proved that those who failed have long ceased to invest in a daily personal time of prayers, scriptural reading and worship Ps 1:1-3.

<u>Live Your Life for People Rather Than Making Life about Yourself- Self-Centred</u>

Jesus lives forever today because he lived for and blessed people Mk 10 and 45.

<u>Maintain moral discipline</u>

Paul told Timothy about moral uprightness in life and ministry

1. Keep yourself

2. Withdraw yourself

3. Save thyself

4. Watch yourself

5. Keep yourself pure

i. <u>Self-Development</u>

One way to keep in tune with our contemporary is through self-development.

Develop your personality

Develop your knowledge

Develop your communication skills

Develop your human relationship

Develop your message delivery

Develop your prayer life

Develop holy living

Develop habits of reading

Develop how to hear from God all the time

Develop your character

j. <u>Develop Your Leadership Skills</u>

The science of leading people is so important that we need to develop and improve on the previous knowledge of leadership. Research have shown the following characteristics as the staying powers for all that remain relevant in generation.

1. A man of knowledge

2. A man of faith

3. A man fired by love

4. A man with God's own mind

5. A true worshippers of God

6. A man who truly serves God not men or material things of life

7. A man who values his salvation

8. A man who truly loves God and Christ

9. A humble man

10. A man who loves God's word

11. A man who is always filled with the spirit of God Ephesians. 5:18

12. A man who sees God and endures affliction or trial

13. A man of prayer

14. A man of sincerity

15. A heavenly minded man Col 3:1-2

16. A patient man. James: 5

17. A zealous man Rom. 12:11

18. A man who loves the saints

19. A man who doesn't indulge in secret sin

20. A man who is good in his relationship with others and God

21. A man who does spiritual things in a spiritual manner

22. A man who is thoroughly trained in the way of God Luke. 6:40

23. A man who walks with God. Genesis 5:

24. A constant soul winner. Daniel 12:3

25. A man who is totally submitted to the will of God

26. A man who walks in obedience to God and Holy Spirit

27. A man who cherishes God's word

28. A man who accepts correction Hebrews. 12:5

29. A man who develops on daily basis

30. A man who fears God

31. A man of humility Philippians. 2:5-11

A man who will remain relevant must do these four things

1. They stay in -   the scriptures Josh 1:8-9, Ps 119:9-11, Ps 1:1-3

2. They stay close - mentor Heb 3:12-3, Prov 27, Iron Sharpeneth iron.

3. They stay away - 2Cor 6:14-18, 2Cor 7:1, 1 John 2:15-17, 1 John 5

4. They stay alert - to the tactics of the enemies 2 Cor 2:11, 1 Pet 5:8

They also avoid doctrinal controversy and walk daily in the fear of God and develop godly character.

CHAPTER SEVEN

RESTORATION FOR THE FALLEN HEROES (HOSEA 6:1-3)

Restoring a backslider is an uphill task (Prob 14:14) how much more helping great heroes of faith who had fallen or left their first love. It will be more tasking; however it is the responsibility of every strong believer (Gal 6:1). It is no news at all that uncountable number of God's lovers, serious minded Christians, holy children and minsters of God have been victims of end-time demonic manipulation and have fallen and have been restored. The possibility of falling is glaringly, clear in the bible.

"if any one thinketh he standeth let him taketh heed lest he falleth" (1Corinthians 10:13, 1John 1:7-9)

Apostle Paul paid serious price to stay put in ministry (1Cor 9:24-27. Severally, he warned Titus and Timothy to take heed or to beware or save thyself and watch yourself. He also predicted that in these last days, there shall be fallen away and loss of first love. We should be thinking of how to restore ourselves rather than arguing unnecessarily the possibility of falling, the restoration of fallen saints is a divine mandate (Gal 6:1, 2Thess 3:15, 1Cor 7:5).

HOW TO RESTORE FALLEN HEROES:

It is an uphill task but the grace of God and determination to help a fallen brother will prepare one's heart against discouragement and despair. t

The principles below will help a long way in solving some problems.

1. Avoid rumours and criticism

2. Avoid superiority complex or 'holier than thee attitude or syndrome'. It could happen to anyone. Experience has shown that those who acted like this in the past eventually ended up the same way.

3. Demonstrate love (John 13:33-35) love is a powerful weapon for the restoration of others.

4. Do not try to convince him/her that she/he does not know what she or he is doing - remember God's word concerning a backslider (Pro 14:14).

5. Be clothed with humility - remember they were once very famous, having seen God's powers, blessing and glory. Trying to tell them anything else will be resisted (1Pet 5:1-6).

6. Learn about how to restore people who have derailed in the faith.

7. Learn about what made him to derail. It could be doctrinal errors, unforgiveness, envy, or problem with immorality? This will help you to tackle them spiritually.

8. Prayers - spiritual warfare has helped so much to restore many big brothers who otherwise could not have been approached.

9. Do not look or talk down on them in the process.

10. Pray for the help, wisdom, and guidance of the Holy Spirit

11. Do not give up because he/she looks down on you

12. Envision the blessing that follows a restorer (James 5:19- 20)

13. Intercede for Him more. 1 Tim 4:16

HOW TO BE RESTORED

Restoring great heroes of faith who once tasted fame and glory, it is a bit difficult except there is willingness on their parts to be restored. The word is "WILLINGNESS" we can only help those who are willing to be helped. Isa 1:19 here are bible procedures that will help whoever is concerned and who has burden to do so.

ON GOD'S SIDE

God wants his servants who have gone astray back to his loving arms. This is seen in the bible where God calls his prodigal servant back to his dear father. **The greatest benefit we all have serving this loving and living God is "mercy". His throne is built on mercy, mercy to the undeserved and unmerited, Hebrews 4:15-16.** There is no limit to what God can forgive, cleanse and reform. Constantly God calls those who have gone astray, promising them abundant forgiveness, restoration and new life Isa 55:6-7. **God has never been hardened to any repentant children or refused them their benefits. When God forgives, he does so completely, without withholding any benefits that accompanied him the first time he was anointed. No one is irredeemable no one beyond the reach of his love, cares and affection no matter how badly one has gone sinking in sin and horrible pit of depravity. No matter how bad one's case might have become, God's grace can handle it 2Cor 12:9-10. The parable of the prodigal son is an epitome of God's** heart for the derailed sons and daughters who once enjoyed his grace and love but squandered it on the altar of prodigality, triviality and wasteful or careless living. The parable of the lost coins and the lost sheep are tremendous exposition on God's longing hearts for the lost servant (Hosea 6:1-3). **God's forgiveness is total.**

No one's case file is closed except when he is in the grave. God's grace and forgiveness is beyond human comprehension. It is incomprehensible and unexplainable. All we can say is that he created and made us sons/daughters and desires that no one should die but come to repentance. When a saint turns to a sinner God's mercy is still opened to him for acceptance (Hosea 6:1-3, Jer 3:10-15). **He made provisions for one's downfall when He planned for salvation** 1John 1:7-9, Heb 4:15-16.

ON PERSONAL LEVEL

1. You must be willing to be restored Isa 1:18-19, God also does not force one against his own wish.

2. Humility – you must accept the fact that you have gone astray – **Manasseh accepted he was wrong 2Chr 33:1-16**

3. Deep repentance and remorse

4. Forsaking and turning away from the past

5. Do not despise the discipline of the Lord Heb 12:5-14

6. Confessing and renouncing wrongs

7. Seeking for cleansing

8. Prayers of repentance

9. Re-adjustment of one's life

10. Begin again

11. Ask for the help of the Holy Ghost Rom 8:17-18

12. Go for counselling

CHAPTER EIGHT

THE CHRISTIAN JOURNEY AND SERVICE AS A RACE

Introduction:

Therefore since we also have such a large crowd of witnesses surrounding us let us lay aside every weight and the sin that so easily besets us, and run with endurance the race that lies before us, keeping our eyes on Jesus, the source and perfecter of our faith, who for the joy that lay before Him endured the cross and despised the shame, and has sat down at the right hand of God's throne. Hebrews 12:1-2 (HCB)

From the writings of Paul it can be concluded that this amazing apostle was many things. He was a missionary, a soul winner, a pastor, a theologian, a tent maker etc but in his spare time he also seemed to be a sport lover. Often in his writing Paul uses sports as an analogy to get his point across. Example: (i) wrestling Eph 6:12 (ii) Boxing 2Tim 4:7, 1Cor 9:26 (iii) Racing 1Cor 9:24; 26.

In our text the apostle chooses to use the analogy of a foot race inferring that the Christian journey can be linked to a race. **The day an individual surrenders his life to Jesus he enters in for this glorious race.**

The object of this race is not to compete with other athletes but rather to please God that enrolled one into the race. **The word of God sets the rule and the standard for this race; to be rewarded one must run according to the rule of the game.** The focus here is how this race relates to the minister and his ministry.

THE RACE AS IT RELATES TO THE MINISTER AND HIS MINISTRY

The Christian journey is a race that every believer enters in for at new birth. Responding to the call of God and the pursuit of the call is another aspect of this race. **The pursuit of the call to ministry like a race has its demands and challenges**, the will of God is that at the end like Paul, each one will be able to say, "I have fought a good fight, I have finished my course. I have kept the faith; henceforth there is laid up for me a crown of righteousness which the Lord, the righteous judge, shall give me at that day... 2Timothy 4:7.

It is important to note that **(i) Not everyone that enters in for a race really finishes (ii) Not all that runs in a race is rewarded (iii) That a man started well is not a guarantee that he shall finish well. Finishing is better than starting** (Ecclesiastes 7:8).

How one starts is important but most importantly is how he finishes, Paul is an example of one that started, finished and now awaits his reward. From the example of the life and ministry of Paul and other Bible characters we shall examine qualities that are required for good finishing.

CERTAINTY OF CALL TO MINISTRY

"And no man taketh this honour unto himself, but he that is called of God, as was Aaron," Hebrew 5:4.

Every child of God has a ministry especially when ministry is viewed as any service the Holy Spirit empowers an individual to carryout to advance God's kingdom on earth. The five-fold ministry according to Eph 4:9-13 is a higher dimension of ministry that no one can afford to dabble into without a deep heart-seated conviction. **Bishop T.D Jakes once said, "If you can avoid ministry, avoid it as much as you can; if you succeed avoiding it, which means you are not called to it".** You don't embark on this kind of journey because someone prophesied to you. You respond to this dimension of ministry based on deep personal persuasion. Until God separates a man into such office he has no business venturing into it. **Paul said, "God called me to preach Him among the**

heathen in Gal 1:15-17". Every other means of guiding may only confirm your inner conviction.

Certainty of call to ministry is as important to ministry as a foundation is to a building. When You miss this aspect everything else that you labour to do, will be labour in futility. **What will keep a man standing in the face of all odds is his conviction that he is where God wants him to be.** Ministry is not of product concern. Moses started with concern and when opposition rose, he ran away, later when God commissioned him for the same assignment, he was able to withstand every opposition. That leads me to conclude that, **when God calls a man he funds him, when a man calls himself he pays his own bill 1Corinthians 9:7. Remember Jonah paid his fare to Tashishi but when he was set to obey God, God miraculously brought him to Nineveh.**

MANAGING DISTRACTION

"Looking unto Jesus the author and finisher of our faith..."

Hebrews 12:2

Ministry is a marathon not a short race. Along the path to the finish line there will be distractions. These distractions could include; (i) the applause / criticism of men (ii) secret envies of progress / successes of others (iii) the unconscious pride that comes from personal progress and (iv) distraction that comes from personal / family needs.

Distraction has remained one of the weapons in the hand of Satan used to try to keep the ministers and believers from being their best for God. From the list above, meeting family/ personal need remains a major area of distraction for most ministries. **Saul, the first monarch of Israel was a man that allowed himself to be distracted by the opinion of the people and thereby lost his throne, 1Samuel, 13:14. When a man gives into distraction in ministry, he begins to sink like Peter who is also an example of a man that yielded to distraction, Matthew 14:30.**

The word of God in Hebrews 12:2 provides solution to the problem of distraction that is, looking unto Jesus…to look any other direction will breed discouragement. The apostle Paul said "…**but this one thing I do, forgetting those things which are behind, and reaching forth unto those things which are before" Philemon 3:13-14.**

HANDLING DISCOURAGEMENT

"…who for the joy that set before him endured the cross, despising the shame…"Hebrew 12:2

Another common challenge on the path of the minister as he presses towards the mark of God's high calling is discouragement. Discouragement is an age –

long weapon in the arsenal of satan. There are a number of examples of men in the scripture who at different stages were faced with discouragement.

Reading through the scripture, you will discover that discouragement is no respecter of title or position. Today, there are so many things the enemy uses to get the minister to be discouraged. **Discouragement could set in when (i) An individual could not attain unrealistic goals in ministry (ii) An individual allows other things apart from Jesus to be his motivation (iii) An individual allows the present challenges to becloud his view of the glory ahead.**

Elijah was a mighty prophet of the Old Testament; the Bible recorded how God mightily used him to bring about a national revival. This is the same man that singlehandedly slay 450 prophets of Baal, but ran away at the threat from Queen Jezebel. His complains afterwards revealed that he was discouraged.

Accounts from lives of David and Paul show how a minister should handle discouragement today. The bible said, *"And David was greatly distressed: for the people spoke of stoning him...but David encourage himself in the Lord"* 1Sam 30:3. Also, concerning Paul it is recorded that he said, *"But none of these things move me neither count my life dear unto myself, so that I might finish my course with joy, and the ministry which I have received of the Lord Jesus"* Acts 20:24.

MANAGING SUCCESS

"But the God of all grace, who hath called us unto his eternal glory by Christ Jesus, after that ye have suffered a while, make ye perfect, establish, strengthen, and settle you". 1Peter 5:10

It does not matter where you are on your journey to the finish line. God's intention is to make you perfect, established, and strengthen so you can finish your course with joy. As in a race and life, there are stages in the pursuit of ministry, at whatever stage, ministry is hard work. A lot of diligence and discipline is required. But while instigating all the time and labour, God has a way of encouraging the minister, with victories and success. **There comes a stage in ministry especially when one has remained faithful following God and heeding His instructions that every little effort seems to bring overwhelming result.**

The greatest temptation at such moment is the tendency to slack at doing those things that are instrumental to the success in the first place.

There are ways to remain relevant in life and ministry is:

1. **Be sensitive to the leading of the Holy Spirit**

2. **Maintaining a teachable heart**

3. **Being flexible to positive change as the Spirit leads**

CHAPTER NINE

<u>TAKE YOUR FAMILY ALONG</u>

"And if it seem evil unto you to serve the Lord, choose you this day whom ye will serve, whether the gods which your fathers served were on the other side of the flood, or the gods of the Amorites, in whose land ye dwell: **BUT AS FOR ME AND MY HOUSE WE WILL SERVE THE LORD**" Joshua 24:15. The joy and fulfilment of life and ministry cannot be full without the family being carried along.

Running alone in ministry that is, doing ministry without one's spouse and children be linked to when a man embarks on a sea journey without the necessary sea fairing facilities and equipment. He may end up swimming instead of having a smooth sail or he may arrive to discover it was a wasted journey.

Scriptures support the view that God sometimes if not all the time, calls families. The example of Moses prophet / leaders of state, Aaron the priest and Miriam the prophetess (all born of the same parents 1Chr 6:3) suffices very well.

When Aaron was called, God made it clear that it was he along with his children that were to be priest, and only descendants of LEVI (His great grandfather) should serve the priests Ex 28:1 and Num 18:1-2.

In Isaiah 59:21 the Lord makes it plain "As for me this is my covenant with them, saith the Lord; my spirit that is upon thee, and my words which I have put in thy mouth, shall not depart out of thy mouth, nor out of thy SEED, nor out of thy seed's saith the LORD from henceforth and forever".

There is certainly the case when others members of family are not called to the pulpit ministry. Then they must be involved in very strategically supportive positions in the work.

When a minister (male or female) runs alone without the immediate family members, one of the dangers is that aloofness is inspired in them. Indifference soon follows. Family members so concerned then see the ministry, its pains, glory, ups downs and all others vicissitudes associated with the work, as the personal business of that ministry. For what is glorious in Glory you cannot share with your loved ones. And how burden-some that you cannot share with loved ones.

If the danger were to end at aloofness and indifference to the ministry, it won't have been alarming. It's the fact that they can be transferred to God and thus leading to complete denying of the faith. What joy and satisfaction is there in winning the world and losing the family?

It's a most blessed and beautiful thing to have your family members with you in either voluntary or official capacities in ministry. The support of family members is all the more so special because it can be taken for granted. They see the work as their own not just the minister's cup of tea. Vision ownership translate into commitment at such a level that such loved ones can make any sacrifice required. Oh! What a joy when this is the case!!

Examples abound from the word of God of those who carried family along and those who didn't. God Himself testified of Abraham in Genesis 18:19 "for I know him, that he will command his children and his household after him and they shall keep the way of the Lord…".

His son of promise Isaac kept the faith, Jacob stayed to the end with God and the nation of Israel today testifies to this.

It could be said that David may not have carried his family along fully. It does not seem evident that his sons were in his army. Absalom was more than an army material, judging from his antecedents not to talk of his older brothers. It does not also seem to be the case that they were involved in administration. The confusion, death and utter disarray that followed, culmination in the understanding end of Solomon and division of the Kingdom may have had their roots in running without the family, of David.

Eli's Case throws up another dimension. It is not enough to run with the family by giving them visible position as was with Hophni and Phineahas but that they be well taught and brought up in the nurture and admonition of the Lord.

Compromising standards can be one of the challenges of involving the family in ministry. Official matters can be easily "emoted" (handled emotional) thus leading to looseness that results in the Hophni and Phineahas syndrome.

Most certainly our song should be "Behold, I and the children whom the Lord hath given me are for signs and for wonders in Israel from the Lord of host, which dwelleth in the mount Zion" Isaiah 8:18. To be relevant in life and ministry you must not run alone. Be sure to involve your family.

DANGERS OF RUNNING WITHOUT THE FAMILY

Unfulfilment in life and ministry often characterised the lives of those who are unable to maintain the delicate balance of success in life, family and ministry. Sadness and Sorrow are often on the same trail many times as in the case of Eli, the tragic end.

Before ministry positions should come the leading of the family to fear and keep the way of the Lord. This is the first ministry.

Eli failed in these regards for scriptures said "Now the sons of Eli were sons of Belial, they knew not the LORD" 1Samuel 2:12. For our family to know the Lord will take some fight, a lot of prayers, plenty of patient teaching, diligent rebuking and faithful believing in God to do it.

The great prophet and priest, Samuel (who also was the human Governor of Israel) also did not succeed with his family. Concerning him Bible says "and his sons walked not in his ways, but turn aside after lucre and took bribes and perverted judgement" 1Samuel 8:3.

The word of God cherishes the minister who "ruleth well his own house, having his children in subjection with all gravity, (for if a man know not

how to rule his own house shall he take care of the church of God)". 1Timothy 3:4-5.

It must be priority of the minister to lead the family to know the Lord and to serve Him. You must win your wife or husband to the ministry. They must be your first and primary workers and helpers. If you are not supporting your husband, you cannot be right nor spirit led. You certainly are against God.

If your wife is the one called and you are not supporting her, you cannot be building with Christ.

As a child it is your duty to follow your parents to serve the Lord. If not your end will be bad and most likely put your parents down to dishonour and failure.

BENEFITS OF CARRYING YOUR FAMILY ALONG

The great benefit is the commendation and joy of the Lord as is obvious from Gen 18:17-19 concerning Abraham. True greatness and might before the Lord is linked to commanding the family to "Keep the way of the Lord". **Oh man of God, do not neglect your wife for she is your greatest insurance, against sex-sin which unarguably is the greatest killer of enduring ministry success. Win her, involve her and humble yourself before her, for the reward of having your wife by your side in ministry cannot be compared to silver or gold. Oh wife, flow with your husband in** ministry. **You are the next helper to him after the Holy Ghost.** Your reward for doing so will be immeasurable. A family well won to the ministry is the truly successful minister's family, there you will find true joy and contentment.

<u>LAST WORDS</u>

Many stories abound from here at home and distance lands, of "great and visible" ministers who lost their children to homosexuality, drugs, crime, substance abuse and all manner of vices. The factors are always the same; busy schedules that allow no time for family; neglect of the spouse, lack of intercession for the family while being a great intercessor for others etc.

The task is clear. We must pray for family to know and serve God. We must do what we can to win them. We must show the example of humility and meekness. Above all we must trust and believe God to help us carry our families along as we obey God in life and ministry.

CHAPTER TEN

<u>CHARACTER: A REQUIREMENT FOR LASTING IN THE MINISTRY INTRODUCTION</u>

"He must be ready to pay the price by being dogged in pleasing heaven, hating with a passion what God hates and fleeing what God forbids. You must hate evil if you love the Lord".

Do you want to fulfil your vision and be fulfilled in that vision and ministry? Do you want to last in the ministry? Or, do you want to rise, then become irrelevant and simply fade away? In this case it will be said or written concerning you that there used to be a powerful man of God who did effective work in ministry for a time but has simply gone into oblivion! God forbid that is not your portion.

However, this can be so concerning you if you do not develop great character. Your ministry can thus be in the classification of the ephemeral. You are therefore:

a) A failure personally

b) A let down in the body of Christ, and

c) A failure in the task assigned to you by God

This therefore means that you have not allowed God to achieve the assigned task through you. The implication is that God will have to equip another servant to salvage the situation. Isn't that a shame? That is the reason it is often said that anointing without character is a disaster. We may capture this in a simple equation thus: Po - Pt =Dt.

Po = Power

Pt = Purity

Dt = Disaster

i.e, power without purity is a disaster.

A minister therefore must develop character of being a God seeker and not a gold seeker and be more interested in making heaven than making a name for himself; focusing and setting affection on things above and not things on the earth Col 3:1-2. He must be ready to pay the price by being dogged in pleasing heaven, hating with a passion what God hates and fleeing what God forbids. You must hate evil if you love the Lord (Ps 97:10).

WHAT IS CHARACTER?

Character is the total quality of a person's behaviour as revealed in many ways including habits of thought and expression, attitudes and interest, actions and philosophy of life. It is the central being of a person which distinguishes him from other individuals and reflects as to how an individual conducts his life.

A woman once described her husband as a man of Belial and that as his name (Nabal) connotes "foolishness is with him" 1Sam 25:25 and in verse 39 we see that "the Lord hath returned the wickedness of Nabal upon his own head.

There are negative character traits that a man who will last in ministry must not accommodate. These include but not limited to the following: Pride, Self-centeredness, Hypocrisy, Enjoying Sin and seeking ways to cover up sin,   lack of compassion for lost souls, lack of urge to grow spiritually being unable to spend quality time with God, tendency to challenge God's authority etc.

The remedy is found in Ps 34:18 "the Lord is nigh unto them that are of a broken heart; and saveth such as be of a contrite spirit". Let us examine briefly one or two exams of character traits.

1. Acknowledge God as your source

From John 15:5 we learn that without the Lord we can do nothing. If therefore through spiritual arrogance you do not acknowledge God as your source, you are heading for destruction.

Are you a minister who has become arrogant in iniquity because you have no respect for God's standards? Do you do what you please and become oblivious or unconcerned that you have slipped into wickedness? For example can you divorce your wife and marry your sin partner declaring that God is a God of a second chance? This would be theology and doctrine of devils directly from hell. **When people begin to praise you and you enjoy it, you are courting trouble. You had better reject the flatteries and instead give all the glory to God. A broken person does not live on the adulation of society.**

I call to witness:

a) Herod who took God's glory (Acts 12:21-23) and was eaten by worms

b) Uzziah – became arrogant when God had helped him tremendously (2Chr 26:16-21) and was struck with leprosy

c) Belshazzar – out of pride desecrated the vessels of the sanctuary and was dazed by a strange vision of a writing on the wall by a part of God's hand. That night he was slain Dan 5.

You should meditate on (Dan 5:23; "...the God in whose hands thy breath is and whose are all thy ways, thou hast not glorified". Pride is a destroyer.

2. Do You Have Integrity

Integrity is moral soundness i.e. conduct or attitude judged from the view point of right and wrong and the distinctions between them.

Do you do right? If for example you have no control over your body, you have no right for spiritual ministry. You will lose respect as no one can trust you in relationships with the opposite sex or financial transactions or doing things properly or appropriately. You must police yourself, check yourself.

Being able to discipline yourself is a hallmark of responsible leadership for we know that all things may be lawful but not all are expedient nor do all things edify 1Corinthians 10:23. As a mobiliser, your speech must be gracious as no corrupt communication should pass through our lips.

We must stay clear of uncouth behaviours and even concerning food let there be dignity.

3. Immediacy Mortgages the Future

Why start a ministry without proper preparation? Why the hurry? Don't you know that the devil promotes in order to destroy? To lead you must go through service and even through servitude (serving like a fool or slave). This is going through God and be assured that those who went through the devil will not become greater eventually. **You should hear from God first, wait and be properly groomed under tutelage for proper preparation.**

Avoid the microwave mentality. Don't you remember that Joshua trained under Moses and Elisha under Elijah, and even Saul, a doctor of law before conversion studied under Gamaliel before his

dramatic encounter on the way to Damascus and still waited to be discipled?

Those under groomed, mushroom pastors are half - baked, lack depth and the essential ingredient of character. This cannot stand any storm and are prone to collapsing under pressure to perform. They are most likely going to seek for power from the wrong source like Saul who went to the witch of Endor? (1Sam 28:7). Lack of proper preparation destroys the future, as the train travels on wobbling wheels.

CHAPTER ELEVEN

<u>WHY DO SOME TRAVELLING MINISTRIES FAIL?</u>

<u>GOD'S call on your life is enough proof that He wants you to succeed. God NEVER calls anyone to fail. If we do ministry God's way, we will not fail.</u>

If you have been called by the Lord into the Ministry, you need to:

i. Find your place

ii. Fit into your place

iii. Function in your place

Not every place is your place. Not every 'vacant' office in the Body of Christ can be filled by just anyone.

God is the one who <u>sets</u> people in offices as he wills 1Corinthians 12:28.

Every man has his <u>proper gift</u> of God, one after this manner, and another after that (1Cor 7:7).

Some ministers have been sent by the owner of the church to pastor churches, but not all. Some have been set in the body of Christ as traveling Ministers.

<u>WHO IS A TRAVELLING MINISTER?</u>

Acts 1:8, Mark 16:15, 3John 1:5-8

1. A travelling minister is an itinerant minister who habitually travels from one church to another. Although he may have a home church where you can trace him to, his primary ministry is not to that local church.

2. He usually would not settle down to pastor a particular church. He moves from place to place as doors of opportunity open.

3. He is often not on the pay roll of a church. His ministry thrives on the honorarium. He receives from invitations or the partners he is able to raise.

4. He is not like a General Overseer that visits other branches under him; he often has a specialised ministry that brings balance or completeness to the Body of Christ e.g. healing crusades, marriage seminars, leadership development, economic empowerment, etc.

5. In the general context, he has no members he can call his own and often has no committed partners. There are no regular Sunday tithes and offerings he can depend upon for the running of his ministry.

This kind of ministry is plagued with peculiar challenges. If these challenges are not overcome, they could stand in the growth of the itinerant ministry.

Challenges of Travelling Ministers

1. **The pressure to do what is popular rather than what is proper – to join the rat race instead of staying in the right race.** The vogue today is to start a church and then open branches. To do something different may make you look like a miss-fit. The fear of being different or the fear of rejection has made many travelling ministers join the 'band wagon' of starting churches. If you insist on wearing shoes that are not your size you will walk funny. You will experience pains. **If you decide to pursue ministry without his grace, you will inevitably end in disgrace.**

2. The unscriptural definition of "success" is causing a lot of problems. It is the reason why some travelling ministers are discouraged. Success in ministry today is defined in terms of:

   a. Size of auditorium

   b. Numerical strength of the Church

   c. Number of branches

   d. The cost of his wardrobe, and a lot of such childishness.

Any travelling minister who accepts such an enormous yardstick for success will become discouraged very fast. He will be tempted to quit the travelling ministry.

3. The poor treatment meted out to travelling ministers by host Pastors. Some Pastors don't know how to appreciate and honour travelling ministers. Even if they can afford it, they do not take good care of itinerant ministers. They don't give wholesome honorarium. **They tend to forget that what they give the travelling minister is what he will use to pay his staff and also meet his family commitments. This is what has led to the unethical practices of ministers charging for their services.**

4. Some Pastors discourage their members from partnering with travelling ministers. They closely monitor their members and express displeasure at members investing in traveling ministries when "there is so much need in the local church".

5. Lack of proper organisation is one reason why travelling ministries are experiencing a hard time. Some travelling ministries lack proper administrative set up. They are unorganised. Some that have been in existence for ten years still run their ministries from their bedrooms. They have no office. Such ministries don't have a future; not in the 21st century.

6. Inadequate preparation for ministry. Most bible schools prepare their students for missions. Those

who end up as travelling ministers just 'stumble into it' with little or no preparation. They are left to learn from their mistakes. Often they have no mentors to learn from.

7. **Inadequate prayer base. No ministry can grow beyond its prayer base. Any ministry whose prayer base is weak is doomed to fail.** Pastors have the advantage of having the whole church praying for them. Some raise special prayer teams within the church to pray consistently for them. What about the travelling ministers? Many depend only on their wives and children to play this most crucial role.

8. The evil practices indulged in by some travelling ministries. This has made it difficult for the genuine ones to be accepted.

i.   Ministers travelling with their female secretaries.

ii. Ministers involved in shameful acts of immorality with church members.

iii. Ministers charging fees before accepting invitations.

iv. Ministers creating doctrinal confusion that leads to church splits.

v.   Ministers who have unethical ways to raise money or partners for themselves.

The list is endless. As a result, certain pastors have closed their doors permanently to travelling ministers.

9. The toll of the travelling ministry on the family. The price some families pay because of the travelling nature of the man is at times great. The responsibility of raising the children is sometimes shouldered alone by the wife. The father is an absentee father. The children grow up to detest the work of the ministry that denied them of their fathers.

10. Travelling ministers are exposed to certain risks. This is the reason why some of them fail e.g. road, or air mishaps, temptation in hotels, temptation from the internet, satellite TV etc. loneliness during travels and attendant risks.

11. Title loving and title curious ministers can never do well as travelling ordained Bishops, Archbishops or Primates, they are referred to as Reverend or Evangelists; at times they are simply called Bro or Uncle.

12. Aging and Job security. When Pastors serve for many years and eventually retire, the churches they served often take care of them in their old age. This is one area of challenge that travelling ministries have to grapple with.

13. The challenge of successor. True success will give birth to a successor. In the church setting this appears much easier. These challenges are no doubt real but not insurmountable. They must not be accepted as reasons for failure. By applying

scriptural wisdom there is a way out. Traveling ministries can also do well.

Why Some Travelling Ministries Do Not Last

1. Lack of integrity
2. Doctrinal controversies
3. Love of money
4. Immorality
5. Lack of knowledge of ministerial ethics
6. Bad human relationships
7. Inter-church crisis
8. Lack of Patience
9. Lack of abiding in one's calling
10. Lack of contentment
11. Lack of knowing divine will of God
12. Lack of Holiness
13. Prayerless life
14. Deviation from original call
15. Poverty
16. Lack of good appreciation by church / ministry. Poor allowance and honorarium

CHAPTER TWELVE

<u>RAISING A WORKFORCE</u>

Every servant of God in the bible took time to raise a strong workforce to accomplish his vision and goals in a recorded time

Mark 3:12-14; 2Tim 4:11

Every minister of God has three important working capitals – among these capitals is **WORKFORCE!**

The matter of raising a workforce in the church or ministry cannot be over emphasised. This is so, because, no ministry is greater than her workforce, strong ministry is a product of strong work force, more so, no ministry can do more exploits than the strength of her workforce, the numerical strength of a church does not determine her quality, usefulness and effectiveness but the workforce. Every servant of God in the bible took time to raise a strong workforce to accomplish his vision and goals in a recorded time. Abraham developed and trained a strong workforce with which he fought his battles (Genesis 14:13-16), Moses did, Joshua did (Josh 1:11 & Josh 4:4). Prophet Samuel did institute three different Bible colleges where he trained prophet to help further the work of God at Jericho, Bethel and Gilga, called sons of prophets. God searches for who to use for his purpose on earth from the time, he began to relate with man, from Genesis to Revelation, God has always been in search of who to use for his work from generation to generation, (Isa 6:6-8, Act 13:22, Ezek 22:29-31). Men have always been God's method to reach the world for Himself; He picked some from quota of life, washed and polished them and his ambassador; He picks prince / princess, educated as well as fools as channels to reach the world. He has power to mould them, to his taste and satisfaction through long training in various manners, directly or indirectly. He picks generals as well as civilians, professionals as well as labourers, the jobless and illiterates are all his delight, He does not look at what they are right now but what they will become here after. He sees potential and possibility in every one; He sees hope and future in the end of everyone, He believes in every one's ability; He sees light at the end of your tunnel. Jesus Christ the son of the living God who came to do the work of Him that send Him decried the abundant availability of God's work and the scarcity of labourers to accomplish the same Matthew 9:8. He then requested, never started his ministry until He had selected and trained the twelve to be with him (Mark 3:12-14).

Every King in the bible selected strong, dynamic and intelligent young men for training to do the followings

    a. To protect the Kingdom

    b. To expand the Kingdom

c. To establish the Kingdom

d. To administer the Kingdom

e. To bring prosperity to the Kingdom

f. Sustain the Kingdom

REFERENCES: (Daniel 1:1-5, 2Cor 4:7, 1Chro 11:9-11, 1Cor 1:26-31, Josh 1:10 and Josh 4:4)

It is a known fact that no minister can single handedly accomplish his vision, he must train people to run with his vision (Hebrews 2:2-2. His workers are his vision runners or vision extenders. Jesus trained some to go where he could not go (Mark 3:13-14).

Every ministry needs the following:
1. Effective workforce (able men) 1Chron 11:9-11

2. Obedience workforce

3. Intelligence workforce

4. Loyal workforce

5. Holy Ghost filled workers John - 15:1-8

6. Fruitful workers - John 15:1-8

7. Men of Faith - Hebrew 11

8. Men of vision - Moses Prov 29:18

9. Men that can be trained, developed and delegated Acts 4:13

10.Men of prayer

11.Humble people – James 4:6

12.Men who are available – Romans 12:1-2,Luke 19

13.Responsible works – 1 Corinthians

14.Faithful and dependable worker 1Cor 4:1-2

15.Profitable workers 11Tim 4:11

16.Trained workforce Luke 6:40

17.Potentially endowed workforce Eph 4:7

18.Committed. Dedicated, consecrated, Holy and prayerful workforce Rom 12:1-2.

19.Men who are willing to be trained

20.Men who loves and could be prepared for service

21.Men who have value for Christian Service

22.Men who are role model

All of the above are products of hard work, prayer and commitment. If all the labourers in your church are not already made effective workers. Your will have to develop them.

I overheard a pastor saying "all you need is anointing", over the years I have been in ministry. **I have come to understand that you need more than anointing to accomplish your God-given vision, though anointing has its powerful roles but raising workforce will enhance your anointing and vision and save you from**

untimely death. The advice of Patriarch Jericho, Moses in-law cannot be ignored. Moreover Christianity has grown in knowledge and understanding to know the indispensability of workforce in ministry (Exodus 18). **We must discard our indispensable mentality and selfish image, Alpha and Omega image we carve, to allow God's divine order take place as God intends his church to be run Eph 4:7-16).** God gives gift to every member of the church, so the minister in charge of God's people must avoid insecurity complex or fear of the unknown, allow and train individuals that could be trained Ephesians 4:7 and Lk 6:40.

REASONS WHY WE RAISE A WORKFORCE

1. It is divine principle – Matt 28:19-20
2. Men were Christ's method to reach the world MK 3:1-14

The question to ask ourselves is what was Christ's Strategy to reach the world of His time and 2000 years after His ascension still reaching the world? "MEN WERE HIS METHOD".

Point 1: He chose men before he started his work (Mk 3:1-14)

Point 2: He trained men for his work (Mk 3:13-14)

Point 3: He gave mandate to pray for labourers 1MH 9:36-38

Point 4: He delegated men (Mk 3:13-14, Lk 10:1-17)

Point 5: He gave power to men to reach the world (Act 1:4-8)

Point 6: He commanded us to raise people (Mtt 28:18-20)

Point 7: He committed the world vision-mandate to men (Mk 16:15)

3. It is the key to do perfect and acceptable service (Rom 12:1-2)

4. To expand your vision (Mtt 28:19-20)

5. To ease the burden of the ministry off the men of God (Act 6:1-4)

6. For church growth (Eph 4:16)

7. To prolong God's work on earth

8. To raise future leaders (2Tim 2:2)

9. To bridge gaps in ministry (Judges 2:10-13, Psalm 78:1)

10. To Produce workforce for the ministry

11. To raise successor (Phil 4:9) etc

Great ministries around us emphasised more on raising future generation leaders and helpers in ministry than preaching and teaching ministry. Many be leaders of tomorrow. The success of your ministry depends largely on this principle while alive and after your transition to glory. It does not have an opinion. **Many ministers would have been successful, effective, lasting and enduring had** they followed this simple divine principle without building the ministry around them as if they will live forever. Raising workforce will help your ministry now and forever. From my observation over the years through past church history and today Pentecostal, it concluded that those who trained and re-trained workers during their life times have more powerful ministry while alive and even more powerful after their demise. While those (penticostal ministry) who built their ministry around themselves due to selfishness and lack of trust in others wasted energy while alive and may be regretting their actions now in paradise "success without a successor is failure" is a popular saying.

The apostle sought for certain quality individual to set over God's work (Act 6:14). Paul the great apostle laboured to raise effective Timothy, Titus and profitable Mark for his vision (Col 4:7-18, Rom 16, 1Cor 16:10, Phil 4:1-3).

Bill Graham, the great world evangelist allude the success of his worldwide famous crusade to "Trained team workers".

A business executive was interviewed recently what was responsible for his rapid success, he also concluded "competent team workers".

Jesus never devoted his time to buying drum sets, or building homes or cathedral -

trying to impress people with artistically designed hall but was at all times engaged in **"BUILDING PEOPLE"**, those men were the ones He handed over his ministry (Matt 28:18-20, Mk 16:15-17, Acts 1:4-8).

CONCLUSION

Because man is indispensable in God's programme, every pastor / leader must be an expert in managing people. This principle is God's principle, and every progress depends on it. It is eternal, when God get the right people, miracles happens 2Chronicles 11:9-11 & 2Samuel 23:8).

Generally speaking, your ministry needs more than general Disciples of Christ. You need men and women you can call your own disciples in ministry. Men and women who believe in you, your call, your vision, your leadership, your administration, your entire goals as given you by God, men and women who believe their destiny is attached to your life and ministry. Men who believe they are called to support you in ministry, who cannot leave you when others are leaving you for greener pastures. Men who could even doubt God if he talks to them different from what they have believed all along. Men who can tolerate your mistakes in life and ministry though not those that can follow you to hell but those that will help your ministry to the end John 6:60-66.

Only diligent, careful recruitment, selection of men for training and retraining will accomplish those noble goals and objective for building a successful ministry. The Lord will help you to accomplish this great vision and mandate of the church.

God bless you and your ministries.

ABOUT THE BOOK

The purpose of this book is to caution all believers that they may be careful so that they don't end in the wilderness. It is our responsibility to ensure that we don't fall from grace to disgrace as we run the race. The purpose of entering every race is to be a winner not a loser. Winning the race of salvation should be the uttermost goal for all vessels of God.

Your ministry needs more than general Disciples of Christ. You need men and women you can call your own disciples in ministry. Men and women who believe in you, your call, your vision, your leadership, your administration, your entire goals as given you by God, men and women who believe their destiny is attached to your life and ministry. Men who believe they are called to support you in ministry, who cannot leave you when others are leaving you for greener pastures. Men who could even doubt God if he talks to them different from what they have believed all along. Men who can tolerate your mistakes in life and ministry though not those that can follow you to hell but those that will help your ministry to the end, John 6:60-66.

Microwave Mentality!

Why start a ministry without proper preparation? Why the hurry? Don't you know that the devil promotes in order to destroy?

You should hear from God first, wait and be properly groomed under tutelage for proper preparation

Avoid the microwave mentality. Don't you remember that Joshua trained under Moses and Elisha under Elijah, and even Saul, a doctor of law before conversion, studied under Gamaliel?

God bless you and your ministries.

CONTACT INFORMATION

Author Dr. Leo Ameh

Senior Pastor, Tele-Evangelist,

All Nations Salvation Assembly (ANSA)

Founder Global Outreach Support (GOS).

Email: dr.leo.ameh@ansaministries.org OR

Email: drleoameh@yahoo.co.uk

www.ansaministries.org

"The greatest benefit we all have serving this loving and living God is "mercy". His throne is built on mercy, mercy to the undeserved and unmerited".

"If you can avoid ministry, avoid it as much as you can; if you succeed avoiding it, which means you are not called to it"

Bishop TD Jakes.

NOTES

NOTES

NOTES

NOTES

NOTES

NOTES

NOTES

NOTES

NOTES

NOTES

NOTES

NOTES

NOTES

NOTES

NOTES

NOTES